Department of Defense
MANUAL

DoD Ammunition and Explosives Safety Standards: Glossary

Department of Defense
MANUAL

NUMBER 6055.09-M, Volume 8
February 29, 2008
Administratively Reissued August 4, 2010
Incorporating Change 1, March 12, 2012

USD(AT&L)

SUBJECT: DoD Ammunition and Explosives Safety Standards: Glossary

References: See Enclosure

V8.1. PURPOSE

V8.1.1. Manual. This Manual is composed of several volumes, each containing its own purpose, and administratively reissues DoD 6055.09-STD (Reference (a)). The purpose of the overall Manual, in accordance with the authority in DoD Directives 5134.01 and 6055.9E (References (b) and (c)), is to establish explosives safety standards (hereafter referred to as "standards") for the Department of Defense.

V8.1.1.1. These standards are designed to manage risks associated with DoD-titled ammunition and explosives (AE) by providing protection criteria to minimize serious injury, loss of life, and damage to property.

V8.1.1.2. Due to the size and complexity of this Manual, alternate paragraph numbering has been approved for use throughout. The initial numeric set (V#) refers to the volume number within the Manual; the second set (E#) refers to the enclosure number; and subsequent numbers refer to the section, paragraph, and subparagraph numbers. If there is no E#, the reference is to a section above the signature of the volume.

V8.1.2. Volume. This Volume contains a complete glossary for Volumes 1 through 7 of DoDM 6055.09-M.

V8.1.2.1. Volume 1 provides general explosives safety information and requirements.

V8.1.2.2. Volume 2 provides criteria for the construction of barricades and explosives facilities, to include criteria for facilities with reduced separation distances.

V8.1.2.3. Volume 3 provides general quantity-distance (QD) criteria for the accidental detonation of hazard division (HD) 1.1 through 1.6 AE, and HD 6.1 items containing toxic chemical agents.

V8.1.2.4. Volume 4 provides QD criteria for airfields and heliports, piers and wharfs, and specific facilities.

V8.1.2.5. Volume 5 provides QD criteria for intentional burning or detonation of AE, storage and operations involving energetic liquids, and underground storage of AE.

V8.1.2.6. Volume 6 provides criteria for contingency operations, toxic chemical munitions and agents, and risk-based siting.

V8.1.2.7. Volume 7 provides criteria for unexploded ordnance, munitions response, waste military munitions, and material potentially presenting an explosive hazard.

V8.2. <u>APPLICABILITY</u>. This Volume:

V8.2.1. Applies to:

V8.2.1.1. OSD, the Military Departments, the Office of the Chairman of the Joint Chiefs of Staff and the Joint Staff, the Combatant Commands, the Office of the Inspector General of the Department of Defense, the Defense Agencies, the DoD Field Activities, and all other organizational entities within the Department of Defense (hereafter referred to collectively as the "DoD Components").

V8.2.1.2. DoD-titled AE wherever it is located.

V8.2.1.3. DoD personnel and property when potentially endangered by known host-nation or off-installation AE hazards.

V8.2.1.4. DoD facilities siting and construction, except as indicated in paragraph V8.2.2.

V8.2.1.5. The evaluation of non-DoD explosives siting submissions on DoD installations (see section V4.E5.21.).

V8.2.2. Provided the documentation requirements of paragraph V8.E2.3.5 are met, does not apply to:

V8.2.2.1. Existing facilities, or those approved for construction under then-current editions of these standards. This exception applies for the balance of the useful lives of such facilities provided:

V8.2.2.1.1. The facility continues to be used for its intended purpose.

V8.2.2.1.2. The explosives safety hazards are not increased.

V8.2.2.1.3. Redesign or modification is not practicable.

V8.2.2.1.4. The quantity of AE cannot be reduced for reasons of operational necessity.

V8.2.2.2. Those planned facilities that do not meet these standards, but have been certified by the Heads of the DoD Components (see section V1.E3.4.) as essential for operational or other compelling reasons.

V8.2.2.3. Other situations that, upon analysis by the Heads of the DoD Components and the Department of Defense Explosives Safety Board (DDESB), are determined to provide the required degree of safety through use of protective construction or other specialized safety features.

V8.3. <u>DEFINITIONS</u>. See Glossary.

V8.4. <u>PROCEDURES</u>. This glossary of terms supports the procedures in Volumes 1 through 7. Criteria provided in this Manual are given in English units (e.g., foot or feet (ft), pounds (lbs), pounds per square inch (psi)), with metric equivalents shown in brackets (e.g., meters (m), kilograms (kg), kilopascals (kPa)).

V8.5. <u>RELEASABILITY</u>. UNLIMITED. This Volume is approved for public release and is available on the Internet from the DoD Issuances Website at http://www.dtic.mil/whs/directives.

V8.6. <u>EFFECTIVE DATE</u>. This Volume is effective upon its publication to the DoD Issuances Website.

Enclosure
    References
Glossary

TABLE OF CONTENTS

ENCLOSURE

REFERENCES

(a) DoD 6055.09-STD, "DoD Ammunition and Explosives Safety Standards," February 29, 2008 (cancelled by Volume 1 of this Manual)

(b) DoD Directive 5134.01, "Under Secretary of Defense for Acquisition, Technology, and Logistics (USD(AT&L))," December 9, 2005

(c) DoD Directive 6055.9E, "Explosives Safety Management and the DoD Explosives Safety Board," August 19, 2005

(d) Subpart EE, parts 260 and 266 of title 40, Code of Federal Regulations

(e) Sections 101 and 2710 of title 10, United States Code

(f) Military Handbook MIL-HDBK-240, "Hazards of Electromagnetic Radiation to Ordnance (HERO) Test Guide," November 1, 2002[1]

(g) Joint Publication 1-02, "Department of Defense Dictionary of Military and Associated Terms," current edition

(h) Military Handbook MIL-HDBK-237D, "Electromagnetic Environmental Effects and Spectrum Supportability Guidance for the Acquisition Process," May 20, 2005[1]

(i) Defense Transportation Regulation 4500.9-R, "Defense Transportation Regulation – Part II, Cargo Movement," June 2008

(j) Section 1521(j)(1) of title 50, United States Code

---

[1] Available from Defense Automated Printing, 700 Robbins Avenue, Philadelphia, PA 19111; Phone: 215-697-2179

GLOSSARY

PART I. ABBREVIATIONS AND ACRONYMS

AAR	after action report
AC	hydrogen cyanide
AE	ammunition and explosives
AEL	airborne exposure limit
AGM	aboveground magazine
AGS	aboveground structure/site
AGS (H)	AGS, heavy wall
AGS (H/R)	AGS, heavy wall and roof
AGS (L)	AGS, light
AIT	automatic identification technology
AM	acquisition manager
ASME	American Society of Mechanical Engineers
ASU	ammunition storage unit
BIP	blow-in-place
BLAHA	basic load ammunition holding area
BLSA	basic load storage area
°C	degrees Celsius
C	distance between cells
CA	chemical agent
CAPA	combat aircraft parking area
CBU	cluster bomb/dispenser unit
CE	conditional exemption
CFR	Code of Federal Regulations
CG	carbonyl dichloride (also known as phosgene), compatibility group
CK	cyanogen chloride
ClF_3	chlorine trifluoride
ClF_5	chlorine pentafluoride
cm	centimeter
cm^2	square centimeter
CSS	chemical safety submission
CWM	chemical warfare material
DDESB	Department of Defense Explosives Safety Board
DERP	Defense Environmental Restoration Program
DMM	discarded military munition
DOT	Department of Transportation
DUSD(I&E)	Deputy Under Secretary of Defense for Installations and Environment
EC	engineering control

ECM	earth-covered magazine
EED	electro-explosive device
E_f	expected fatalities
EID	electrically initiated device
EIDS	extremely insensitive detonating substance
ELCG	energetic liquid compatibility group
EME	electromagnetic environment
EMR	electromagnetic radiation
EOD	explosive ordnance disposal
EQN	equation
ES	exposed site
ESM	explosives safety management
ESQD	explosives safety quantity-distance
ESS	explosives safety submission
°F	degrees Fahrenheit
FAA	Federal Aviation Administration
FARP	forward arming and refueling point
ft	foot or feet
ft^2	square foot or square feet
ft^3	cubic feet
FUDS	formerly used defense site
GA	dimethylaminoethoxy-cyanophosphine oxide (common name is tabun) (nerve agent)
GB	isopropyl methylphosphonofluoridate (common name is sarin) (nerve agent)
GD	pinacolyl methylphosphonofluoridate (common name is soman) (nerve agent)
GF	o-cyclohexyl methylphosphonofluoridate (common name is cyclosarin) (nerve agent)
GSA	General Services Administration
H_2O_2	hydrogen peroxide
HAN	hydroxyl ammonium nitrate
HAS	hardened aircraft shelter
HBESL	health-based environmental screening level
HC	hexachlorethane
HD	hazard division
HDD	hazardous debris distance
HE	high explosive
HERO	hazards of electromagnetic radiation to ordnance
HEW	high explosive weight
HFD	hazardous fragment distance
H/HD	2,2' dichlorodiethyl sulfide (common name is distilled mustard) (blister agent)

H/HT	60% HD and 40% 2,2' dichloroethylthiodiethyl ether (common name is mustard-T mixture) (blister agent)
HMX	cyclotetramethylene-tetranitramine
HPM	high-performance magazine
HWCL	hazardous waste control limit
IA	installation activity
IAW	in accordance with
IBD	inhabited building distance
IHF	interim holding facility
ILD	intraline distance
IMD	intermagazine distance
ips	inches per second
IRFNA	inhibited red fuming nitric acid
ISO	International Standardization Organization
J	joule
JHCS	joint hazard classification system
JP	jet propellant
JTF	joint task force
K	factor (also called K-factor) in the English system
kg	kilogram
K_m	value of K in the metric system
kPa	kilopascal
kph	kilometers per hour
kV	kilovolt
kW	kilowatt
L	dichloro (2-chlorovinyl) arsine (common name is lewisite) (blister agent)
lbs	pounds
LH_2	liquid hydrogen
LO_2	liquid oxygen
LPS	lightning protection system
LUC	land use control
M	distance between modules
m	meter
m^2	square meter
m^3	cubic meter
MC	munitions constituent
MCE	maximum credible event
MDAS	material documented as safe
MDEH	material documented as an explosive hazard
MEC	munitions and explosives of concern
MFD	maximum fragment distance

mg	milligram
MGFD	munition with the greatest fragmentation distance
mg-min	milligrams per minute
MIL-STD	Military Standard
mm	millimeter
MMH	monomethylhydrazine
MON	mixed oxides of nitrogen
MOOTW	military operations other than war
mph	miles per hour
MPPEH	material potentially presenting an explosive hazard
MPS	maritime prepositioning ship
MR	munitions rule
MRA	munitions response area
MRC	multiple round container
MRS	munitions response site
ms	millisecond
MSD	minimum separation distance
MWD	military working dog
MWR	morale, welfare, and recreation
N_2H_4	hydrazine
N_2O_4	nitrogen tetroxide
NDAI	no DoD action indicated
NEC	National Electrical Code
NEQ	net explosive quantity
NEW	net explosive weight
NEWQD	net explosive weight for quantity-distance
NFPA	National Fire Protection Association
NIOSH	National Institute of Occupational Safety and Health
NOFA	no further action
NPW	net propellant weight
OB	open burning
OD	open detonation
OSHA	Occupational Safety and Health Administration
P	pad size
PAED	public access exclusion distance
Pa-s	Pascal-seconds
PBAN	polybutadiene-acrylic acid-acrolyonitrile
PES	potential explosion site
PETN	pentaerythritol tetranitrate
P_f	probability of fatality
PM	program manager
POV	privately owned vehicle
PPE	personal protective equipment

psi	pounds per square inch
PTR	public traffic route
PTRD	public traffic route distance
PWP	plasticized white phosphorus
Q	net explosive quantity in kilograms
QA/QC	quality assurance and quality control
QD	quantity-distance
RCRA	Resource Conservation and Recovery Act
RCS	report control symbol
RCWM	recovered chemical warfare material
RDX	cyclotrimethylenetrinitramine (also known as cyclonite, hexogen, or royal demolition explosive)
RF	radio frequency
RFID	radio frequency identification
RORO	roll-on/roll-off
RP	rocket propellant
RSP	render safe procedure
s	second
SAFER©	Safety Assessment for Explosives Risk
SCBA	self-contained breathing apparatus
SD	sympathetic detonation
SDW	substantial dividing wall
SG	sensitivity group
SOP	standard operating procedure
STEL	short-term exposure limit
TCRA	time critical removal action
TEA	triethyl aluminum
TNT	trinitrotoluene
TPA	thickened triethyl aluminum
TSD	team separation distance
TWA	time-weighted average
UDMH	unsymmetrical dimethylhydrazine
UN	United Nations
USACE	U.S. Army Corps of Engineers
U.S.C.	United States Code
USD(AT&L)	Under Secretary of Defense for Acquisition, Technology, and Logistics
UXO	unexploded ordnance
VX	0-ethyl S-[2-(diisopropylamino) ethyl] methylphosphonothioate (nerve agent)

w   loading density
WP   white phosphorus

PART II. DEFINITIONS

Unless otherwise noted, these terms and their definitions are for the purpose of this Manual.

aboveground magazine (AGM). Any open area, vehicle, or any aboveground structure not meeting the requirements of an earth-covered magazine (ECM) that is used for explosives storage.

aboveground structure/site (AGS). Any aboveground, non-earth-covered structure and/or site.

acceptor and donor. A total quantity of stored AE may be subdivided into separate storage units in order to reduce the maximum credible event (MCE). The separation distances between separate storage units, with or without an intervening barrier, need to be sufficient (e.g., intermagazine distance (IMD)) ensuring that propagation between units does not occur. The storage unit that reacts initially is termed the donor and nearby units, which may be endangered, are termed acceptors.

action level. One-half of the exposure limit for a chemical agent averaged over an 8-hour work shift.

active installation. A military installation that is currently in service and being regularly used for military activities.

administration area. The area containing administrative buildings that support the installation as a whole, excluding those offices located near and directly serving AE storage and operating areas.

AE. Includes, but is not necessarily limited to, all items of U.S.-titled (i.e., owned by the U.S. Government through the DoD Components) ammunition; propellants, liquid and solid; pyrotechnics; high explosives (HEs); guided missiles; warheads; devices; and chemical agent substances, devices, and components presenting real or potential hazards to life, property, and the environment. Excluded are wholly inert items and nuclear warheads and devices, except for considerations of storage and stowage compatibility, blast, fire, and nonnuclear fragment hazards associated with the explosives. (See military munitions.)

AE aircraft cargo area Any area specifically designated for aircraft loading or unloading of transportation-configured AE or parking aircraft loaded with transportation-configured AE.

AE area. An area specifically designated and set aside from other portions of an installation for the development, manufacture, testing, maintenance, storage, or handling of AE.

AE facility. Any structure or location containing AE. (Formerly called explosives facility.)

AGS (II). AGS with a wall thickness of 12 inches [304.8 mm] or more of reinforced concrete; as an ES, door must be barricaded if it faces a PES.

AGS (HR). AGS with a wall thickness of 12 inches [304.8 mm] or more of reinforced concrete and a roof thickness of more than 5.9 inches [149.9 mm] of reinforced concrete; as an ES, door must be barricaded if it faces a PES; side/rear exposures may or may not be barricaded.

AGS (L). AGS that is a light structure, open stack, truck, trailer, or railcar.

airborne exposure limit (AEL). Time-weighted averages or ceiling values that define the permissible limits of toxic chemical agent exposure for unprotected personnel.

aircraft passenger transport operations. Passenger transport operations are defined for the purposes of QD as follows: Passenger transport traffic involving military dependents and civilians other than those employed by or working directly for the DoD Components. The following are not considered passenger transport operations: infrequent flights of base and command administrative aircraft that may, on occasion, provide some space available travel to authorized personnel; travel of direct hire appropriated funds personnel employed by any DoD Component; travel of such personnel as contractor and technical representatives traveling to or from direct support assignments at DoD installations.

ammunition. Generic term related mainly to articles of military application consisting of all kinds of bombs, grenades, rockets, mines, projectiles, and other similar devices or contrivances.

ammunition storage unit (ASU). All types of explosives storage magazines; e.g., open storage areas, sheds, bunkers, ECM, and AGM.

anchorages

   scuttling site. A designated area of water for positioning a ship for its flooding or sinking under emergency situations.

   explosives anchorage. A designated area of water used for AE loading and unloading of vessels and for anchoring vessels carrying a cargo of AE.

anomaly avoidance. Techniques employed on property known or suspected to contain unexploded ordnance (UXO), other munitions that may have experienced abnormal environments (e.g., discarded military munition (DMM)), munitions constituents in high enough concentrations to pose an explosive hazard, or CA, regardless of configuration, to avoid contact with potential surface or subsurface explosive or CA hazards, to allow entry to the area for the performance of required operations.

auxiliary building. Any building, e.g., power plant, change house, paint and solvent locker, and similar facilities, related to or maintained and operated to serve an operating building, line, plant, or pier area. AE is not present in an auxiliary building.

barge piers. Piers and wharves used exclusively for loading and/or unloading explosives on barges or utility craft.

barge units. See ship or barge units.

barricade. An intervening natural or artificial barrier of such type, size, and construction that limits the effect of an explosion on nearby buildings or exposures in a prescribed manner.

barricaded open storage module. A series of connected, barricaded cells with hard surface storage pads.

blast impulse. The area under the positive phase of the overpressure-time curve.

blast overpressure. The pressure above ambient in a shock wave.

bonding. A physical and electrical connection between a metal object and the lightning protection sysem (LPS). This produces electrical continuity between LPS and the object and minimizes electromagnetic potential differences. Bonding is done to prevent side-flash. Methods of bonding include mechanical, compression, and thermal types.

break room. A room in an operating building or a separate facility used by personnel to take breaks and eat meals.

bunker suit. Apparel that consists of trousers or overalls tucked into a pair of boots; it is designed for dressing quickly when answering an alarm.

burning reaction. The energetic material ignites and burns non-propulsively. The case may open, melt, or weaken sufficiently to rupture nonviolently, allowing mild release of combustion gases. Debris primarily remains within the area of the reaction. The debris is not expected to cause fatal wounds to personnel or be a hazardous fragment beyond 50 ft [15.2 m].

CA. A chemical compound (to include experimental compounds) that, through its chemical properties, produces lethal or other damaging effects on human beings, and is intended for use in military operations to kill, seriously injure, or incapacitate persons through its physiological effects. Excluded are research, development, test, and evaluation solutions; riot control agents; chemical defoliants and herbicides; smoke and other obscuration materials; flame and incendiary materials; and industrial chemicals.

CA hazard. A condition where danger exists because CA is present in a concentration high enough to present potential unacceptable effects (e.g., death, injury, damage) to people, operational capability, or the environment.

CA safety A condition where operational capability and readiness, people, property, and the environment are protected from the unacceptable effects or risks of a mishap involving chemical warfare material (CWM) and CA in other than munitions configurations.

catenary LPS. An LPS consisting of one or more overhead wires suspended from poles connected to a grounding system via down conductors. The objective is to intercept lightning flashes and provide a zone of protection.

cavern storage site. A natural or manmade cavern adapted for the storage of AE.

ceiling value. The concentration of chemical agent that may not be exceeded for any period of time.

chain of custody. From the time of collection through release from DoD control, the procedures and their implementation, including documentation, marking, and securing, that maintain positive control of material potentially presenting an explosive hazard (MPPEH), material documented as an explosive hazard (MDEH), and material documented as safe (MDAS).

chamber storage site. An excavated chamber or series of excavated chambers especially suited to the storage of AE. A cavern may be subdivided or otherwise structurally modified for use as a chamber storage site.

classification yard. A railroad yard used for receiving, dispatching, classifying, and switching of cars.

closure block. A protective construction feature designed to seal the entrance tunnel to an underground storage chamber in the event of an explosion within the chamber.

cluster bomb/dispenser unit (CBU) military munitions. CBU weapons that are designed to carry and dispense submunitions. (See also sensitivity group (SG)). For purposes of determining case fragment distances for intentional detonations, these military munitions are considered as non-robust munitions.

cold iron. The status of a ship that has shut down its main power plant and is dependent on shore power. A ship in cold iron is not capable of providing immediate propulsion.

combat aircraft parking area. Any area specifically designated for aircraft loading or unloading of combat-configured munitions or parking aircraft loaded with combat-configured munitions.

combustible construction. Construction that uses materials that readily ignite and burn when exposed to fire (e.g., wood frame structures).

compatibility. AE are considered compatible if they may be stored or transported together without significantly increasing either the probability of an accident or, for a given quantity, the magnitude of the effects of such an accident.

compatibility group (CG). Letter designation assigned to AE to indicate what may be stored or transported together without significantly increasing either the probability of an accident or, for a given quantity, the magnitude of the effects of such an accident.

conditional exemption (CE). An exemption from the regulatory definition of hazardous waste (and therefore from compliance with specific environmental requirements pertaining to the storage of hazardous waste) conditioned on compliance with certain criteria requirements, as in part 266.205 of title 40, Code of Federal Regulations (CFR) (Reference (d)).

conductor. An LPS component designed to transfer the current of a lightning flash to the earth electrode system. Conductors are usually heavy metallic cables. However, metallic building structural members (e.g., steel I-beams) can also function as conductors.

connected-chamber storage site. A chamber storage site consisting of two or more chambers connected by ducts or passageways. Such chambers may be at the ends of branch tunnels off a main passageway.

constriction. Short lengths of tunnel whose cross-sectional areas are reduced to one-half or less of the normal tunnel cross-section. Constrictions reduce the airblast effects passing through them. To be effective, constrictions should be placed within five tunnel diameters of the tunnel exit or to the entrances of storage chambers.

construction support. Assistance provided by DoD explosive ordnance disposal (EOD) or UXO-qualified personnel and/or by personnel trained and qualified for operations involving CA, regardless of configuration, during intrusive construction activities on property known or suspected to contain UXO, other munitions that may have experienced abnormal environments (e.g., DMM), munitions constituents in high enough concentrations to pose an explosive hazard, or CA, regardless of configuration, to ensure the safety of personnel or resources from any potential explosive or CA hazards.

container. A package designed to protect AE from hazardous environments during transportation and storage.

counterpoise. A type of an earth electrode system consisting of conductor cables buried around the structure to be protected. Generally, a counterpoise will have more surface area contacting the earth than ground rod systems.

CWM. Items generally configured as a munition containing a chemical compound that is intended to kill, seriously injure, or incapacitate a person through its physiological effects. CWM includes V- and G-series nerve agents or H-series (mustard) and L-series (lewisite) blister agents in other-than-munition configurations; and certain industrial chemicals (e.g., hydrogen cyanide (AC), cyanogen chloride (CK), or carbonyl dichloride (called phosgene or CG)) configured as a military munition. Due to their hazards, prevalence, and military-unique application, CA identification sets are also considered CWM. CWM does not include: riot control devices; chemical defoliants and herbicides; industrial chemicals (e.g., AC, CK, or CG) not configured as a munition; smoke and other obscuration producing items; flame and incendiary producing items; or soil, water, debris or other media contaminated with low concentrations of chemical agents where no CA hazards exist.

CWM response. Munitions responses and other responses to address the chemical safety; explosives safety, when applicable; human health; or environmental risks presented by CA-filled munitions and CA in other than munitions configurations. (See munitions response.)

debris. Any solid particle thrown by an explosion or other strong energetic reaction. For aboveground explosions, debris refers to secondary fragments. For explosions in underground facilities, debris refers to both primary and secondary fragments.

debris trap. A protective construction feature in an underground facility designed to capture fragments and debris from an explosion within the facility.

defense sites. Defined in section 2710(e)(1) of title 10, United States Code (U.S.C.) (Reference (e)).

definitive drawing. A design (e.g., a control bunker, a 3- or 7-Bar ECM, a missile test cell, or a barricade) that has been documented by a DoD Component on numbered drawings approved by the DDESB. The purpose of a definitive drawing is to provide a standard design to ensure consistency in construction. Upon approval by the DDESB, it is not necessary for the definitive drawing to be reviewed again if the design has not been changed.

deflagration reaction. Ignition and rapid burning of the confined energetic materials builds up high local pressures leading to nonviolent pressure release as a result of a low strength case or venting through case closures (e.g., loading ports or fuze wells). The case might rupture but does not fragment; closure covers might be expelled, and unburned and burning energetic materials might be thrown about and spread the fire. Propulsion might launch an unsecured test item, causing an additional hazard. No blast or significant fragmentation damage to the surroundings is expected, only heat and smoke damage from the burning explosive substances.

detonation reaction. A supersonic decomposition reaction propagates through the energetic materials and produces an intense shock in the surrounding medium and very rapid plastic deformation of metallic cases, followed by extensive fragmentation. All energetic materials will be consumed. Effects will include large ground craters for items on or close to the ground; holing, plastic flow damage, and fragmentation of adjacent metal structures; and blast overpressure damage to nearby structures.

disposal. End-of-life tasks or actions for residual materials resulting from demilitarization or disposition operations.

disposition. Reusing, recycling, converting, redistributing, transferring, donating, selling, demilitarizing, treating, destroying, or fulfilling other life-cycle guidance, for DoD property subject to these standards.

dividing wall. A wall designed to prevent, control, or delay propagation of a reaction involving AE on opposite sides of the wall.

DMM. See section 2710(e)(2) of Reference (e). Generally, military munitions that have been abandoned without proper disposal or removed from storage in a military magazine or other storage area for the purpose of disposal. The term does not include unexploded ordnance, military munitions that are being held for future use or planned disposal, or military munitions that have been properly disposed of, consistent with applicable environmental laws and regulations.

<u>documentation of the explosives safety status of material</u>

Documentation attesting that material:

Does not present an explosive hazard and is consequently safe for unrestricted transfer within or release from DoD control, or

Is MPPEH, with the known or suspected explosive hazards stated, that is only transferable or releasable to a qualified receiver.

This documentation must be signed by a technically qualified individual with direct knowledge of:

The results of both the material's 100 percent inspection and 100 percent re-inspection or of the approved process used and the appropriate level of re-inspection, and

The veracity of the chain of custody for the material.

This signature is followed by the signature of another technically qualified individual who inspects the material on a sampling basis (sampling procedures are determined by the DoD entity that is inspecting the material).

<u>DoD explosives operations and/or storage</u>. Explosives operations *that are* conducted *in compliance with the explosives safety standard of this Manual* by the Department of Defense, or *an*other Federal agency *or contractor*, under DoD ~~oversight, procedure, or~~ control *or oversight, and the explosives safety standards of this Manual.* This term is applicable only to DoD and Federal explosives operations and to non-DoD commercial enterprises directly supporting ~~DoD and Federal explosives contractual efforts~~ *such operations under contract, including cases where the actions of a single crew or operating line produces material procurable by either DoD or a non-DoD entity or where ownership of the product changes during the process.*

<u>donor and acceptor</u>. See acceptor and donor.

<u>down conductor</u>. See conductor.

<u>dunnage</u>. Inert material associated with the packaging, containerization, blocking, and bracing of AE.

<u>earth electrode system</u>. An LPS component used for transferring current from a lightning flash to the earth. The earth electrode system (e.g., ground rods, counterpoise, buried metal plates, or Ufer grounds) is connected to down conductors and is in direct contact with the earth.

ECM. An aboveground, earth-covered structure that meets soil cover depth and slope requirements of this Manual. ECMs have three possible strength designations: 7-Bar, 3-Bar, or Undefined. The strength of an ECM's headwall and door determines its designation.

electrically initiated device (EID). Defined in Military Handbook MIL-HDBK-240 (Reference (f)).

electro-explosive device. Defined in Joint Publication 1-02 (Reference (g)).

electromagnetic environment (EME). Defined in Military Handbook MIL-HDBK-237D (Reference (h).

electromagnetic environmental effects. Defined in Reference (f).

electromagnetic radiation. Defined in Reference (g).

emergency withdrawal distance. The distance personnel are evacuated to from an exposed site (ES) during an explosive accident or incident.

emission control. Defined in Reference (g).

energetic liquid. A liquid, slurry, or gel consisting of or containing an explosive, oxidizer, fuel, or their combination that may undergo, contribute to, or cause rapid exothermic decomposition, deflagration, or detonation.

engineering controls. The management of facility operations using engineering principles (e.g., facility design, operation sequencing, equipment selection, or process limitations).

environmental regulators and safety officials. Includes, but may not be limited to, environmental regulators, environmental coordinators, or hazardous material coordinators, law enforcement officers, and safety personnel of the U.S. Environmental Protection Agency, State, interstate, and local governments (which may include Federally recognized Indians tribes and Alaska Native entities), and other Federal land managers. When appropriate, public health officials of various agencies may also be involved.

EOD. The detection, identification, onsite evaluation, rendering safe, recovery, and final disposal of unexploded ordnance and of other munitions that have become an imposing danger, for example by damage or deterioration.

EOD personnel. Military personnel who have graduated from the Naval School, Explosive Ordnance Disposal; are assigned to a military unit with a Service-defined EOD mission; and meet Service and assigned unit requirements to perform EOD duties. EOD personnel have received specialized training to address explosive and certain CA hazards during both peacetime and wartime. EOD personnel are trained and equipped to perform render safe procedures (RSP) on nuclear, biological, chemical, and conventional munitions, and on improvised explosive devices.

EOD unit. A military organization constituted by proper authority; manned with EOD personnel; outfitted with equipment required to perform EOD functions; and assigned an EOD mission.

equivalent explosive weight. The weight of trinitrotoluene (TNT) required to produce a selected shockwave parameter of equal magnitude at a specific location to that produced by a unit weight of the explosive in question.

ES. A location exposed to the potential hazardous effects (e.g., blast, fragments, debris, or heat flux) from an explosion at a potential explosion site (PES).

ES group. Those ESs out to a distance from the PES where contributions to individual risks are no longer significant (i.e., out to the risk-based evaluation distance). (See risk-based evaluation distance.)

essential personnel. Individuals, as identified by the DoD Component, associated with an AE operation.

exemption. A written authorization granted by the proper authority within a DoD Component for strategic or other compelling reasons that permits a long-term deviation from a mandatory requirement of DoD explosives safety criteria.

expansion chamber. A protective construction feature in an underground storage facility designed to reduce the overpressure exiting the facility by increasing the total volume of the tunnel chamber complex. It may also function as an operating area within the underground facility or as a debris trap.

explosion reaction. Ignition and rapid burning of the confined energetic materials builds up high local pressures leading to breakup of the confining structure. Metal cases are fragmented (e.g., brittle fracture) into large pieces that are often thrown long distances. Unreacted or burning energetic materials are also thrown about. Fire and smoke hazards will exist. Air shocks are produced that can cause damage to nearby structures. The blast and high velocity fragments can cause minor ground craters and damage (e.g., breakup, tearing, gouging) to adjacent metal plates. Blast pressures are lower than for a detonation reaction.

explosive. For the purposes of these standards, a substance or a mixture of substances that is capable by chemical reaction of producing gas at such temperature, pressure, and speed as to cause damage to the surroundings. The term "explosive" includes all substances variously known as HEs and propellants, together with igniters, primers, initiators, and pyrotechnics (e.g., illuminant, smoke, delay, decoy, flare, and incendiary compositions).

explosive accident. Accidents resulting in damage or injury from:

An explosion or functioning of explosive materials or devices (except as a result of enemy action).

Inadvertent actuation, jettisoning and releasing, or launching explosive devices.

Impacts of ordnance off-range.

explosive hazard. A condition where danger exists because explosives are present that may react (e.g., detonate, deflagrate) in a mishap with potential unacceptable effects (e.g., death, injury, damage) to people, property, operational capability, or the environment.

explosives or munitions emergency response. Defined in part 260.10 of Reference (d).

explosives safety. A condition where operational capability and readiness, people, property, and the environment are protected from the unacceptable effects or risks of potential mishaps involving DoD military munitions or other encumbering explosives or munitions.

explosives safety management. A cost-effective risk management process, including policies, procedures, standards, engineering, and resources, that addresses potential probabilities and consequences of mishaps involving DoD military munitions or other encumbering explosives or munitions, to sustain operational capabilities and readiness and to protect people, property, and the environment.

extremely heavy case munitions. Military munitions having a cylindrical section case weight to explosive weight ratio greater than 9. Examples of extremely heavy case munitions are 16-inch projectiles and most armor piercing projectiles. (See the Fragmentation Database located on the DDESB secure Web page to determine if a specific item is an extremely heavy case munition.) For purposes of determining sensitivity group (SG), extremely heavy case munitions are considered as robust munitions.

extremely insensitive detonating substance. A substance that, although capable of sustaining a detonation, has demonstrated through tests that it is so insensitive that there is a very low probability of accidental initiation.

Faraday cage. An LPS where the area to be protected is enclosed by a heavy metal screen (similar to a birdcage) or continuous metallic structure with no unbonded metallic penetrations. Lightning current flows on the exterior of the structure, not through its interior.

Faraday-like shield. An LPS that is not an ideal Faraday cage, but is formed by a contiguous conductive matrix that is properly bonded and grounded (e.g., electrically continuous steel arches and reinforcing bars of concrete end-walls and floors of steel arch magazines, reinforcing bars of ECM, or the metal shell of prefabricated "portable" magazines and metal buildings).

firebrand. A burning or hot projection that may transfer thermal energy to the surroundings.

formerly used defense site (FUDS). Properties previously owned, leased, or otherwise possessed by the United States and under the jurisdiction of the Secretary of Defense.

<u>forward arming and refueling point (FARP)</u>. A temporary facility, organized, equipped, and deployed to provide fuel and AE necessary to support aviation maneuver units in combat. The FARP permits combat aircraft to rapidly refuel and rearm and is normally located in the main battle area closer to the area of operation than the aviation unit's combat service area.

<u>fragmentation</u>. Fracture of AE confining cases and structures as the result of an initiation.

<u>fragmenting military munitions</u>. Military munitions having cases that are designed to fragment (e.g., naturally fragmenting warheads, continuous rod warheads, items with scored cases, and military munitions that contain pre-formed fragments). (See also SG.) For purposes of determining case fragment distances for intentional detonations, these military munitions are considered as robust munitions.

<u>frost line</u>. The depth to which frost will penetrate soil (region-dependent).

<u>general public</u>. Persons not associated with a DoD installation's mission or operations (e.g., visitors, guests of personnel assigned to the installation, or persons not employed or contracted by the Department of Defense or the installation).

<u>grounding</u>. The method used for providing an electrical path to the earth or to the earth electrode system. Good grounding is a function of the earth itself; temperature and moisture condition; an ionizing medium such as naturally occurring salts; or the volume of the earth electrode.

<u>ground shock</u>. Coupling of energy to the ground as a result of an AE reaction. Localized movement of the ground or structures in the vicinity will occur.

<u>hardened aircraft shelter (HAS)</u>. A structure designed to minimize aircraft QD separation distances and yet provide a high level of aircraft protection. Defined as being one of these structure types addressed by this Manual:

  <u>First Generation</u>

    <u>TAB VEE</u>. 24-ft [7.3 m] radius semicircular arch, 48-ft [14.7 m] wide by 100.8-ft [30.7 m] long. Double corrugated steel liner covered by a minimum of 18 inches [45.7 centimeters (cm)] of reinforced concrete cover. Front closure is prow-shaped and is produced when two vertically hinged, recessed doors come together. (The closure is recessed approximately 20 ft [6.1 m] from the front of the arch, which provides a smaller internal space for aircraft.) 24-inch [61.0 cm] thick reinforced concrete rear wall, with an interior 0.1255-inch [0.3188 cm] thick steel spall plate. Rear wall has an exhaust opening (normally closed) for venting when engines are running. (Also known as a USAFE TAB VEE.)

    <u>TAB VEE Modified</u>. 24-ft [7.3 m] radius semicircular arch, 48-ft [14.7 m] wide by 100.8-ft [30.7 m] long. Double corrugated steel liner covered by a minimum of 18 inches [45.7 cm] of reinforced concrete cover. Front closure is prow-shaped, laterally opening, external flush door. 24-inch [61.0 cm] thick reinforced concrete rear wall, with an interior 0.1255-inch [0.3188 cm] thick steel spall plate. Rear wall has an exhaust opening (normally closed) for venting when

engines are running. (Same design as TAB VEE, except front closure door is redesigned and relocated to outside of arch.)

Second Generation. 29.4-ft [9.0 m] double-radius, pseudo-elliptical arch; 82-ft [25 m] wide by 124-ft [37.8 m] long. Double corrugated steel liner covered by a minimum of 18 inches [45.7 cm] of reinforced concrete cover. Front closure is a vertical reinforced concrete panel, laterally opening, sliding, external flush door. 24-inch [61.0 cm] thick reinforced concrete rear wall, with an interior 0.1255-inch [0.3188 cm] thick steel spall plate. Rear wall has an exhaust opening (normally closed) for venting when engines are running.

Third Generation. 27.4-ft [8.4 m] double-radius, pseudo-elliptical arch; 70.8-ft [21.6 m] wide by 120-ft [36.6 m] long. Double corrugated steel liner covered by a minimum of 18 inches [45.7 cm] of reinforced concrete cover. Front closure is a vertical reinforced concrete panel, laterally opening, sliding, external flush door. A personnel door is located out one side and is protected by a barricade. 24-inch [61.0 cm] thick reinforced concrete rear wall, with an interior 0.1255-inch [0.3188 cm] thick steel spall plate. Rear wall has an exhaust opening (normally closed) for venting when engines are running.

Korean TAB VEE. 24-ft [7.3 m] radius semicircular arch, 48-ft [14.7 m] wide by 100.8-ft [30.7 m] long (same dimensions and arch design as a First Generation). Double corrugated steel liner covered by a minimum of 18 inches [45.7 cm] of reinforced concrete cover. Either no front closure, or a non-hardened front closure. 18-inch [45.7 cm] thick reinforced concrete rear wall, with a 10-gauge (0.1382-inch) [3.51 millimeters (mm)] steel liner. Rear wall has an exhaust opening (normally closed) for venting when engines are running; exhaust opening is protected only by an exterior blast deflector earth-filled steel bin barricade.

Korean TAB VEE Modified. Same as a Korean TAB VEE, except a First Generation TAB VEE or TAB VEE Modified hardened front closure has been installed.

Korean Flow-Through. 27.4-ft [8.4 m] double-radius, pseudo-elliptical arch; 70.8-ft [21.6 m] wide by 120-ft [36.6 m] long (same dimensions and arch design as a Third Generation). Double corrugated steel liner covered by a minimum of 18 inches [45.7 cm] of reinforced concrete cover. Has an open front and rear.

HAS Pair. Two side-by-side HAS with a First, Second, or Third Generation arch design, separated by a minimum 6-inch [15.24 cm] air gap. The design may be a flow-through, or may have a rear wall, or a front and rear wall.

Maintenance HAS. A First, Second, or Third Generation HAS used for nonexplosive combat aircraft maintenance operations.

HAS ready service ECM/AGM. Facility intended to provide a holding area between HASs for quick-turn munitions. Limited to 22,000 lbs [9,979 kg] net explosive weight for quantity-distance (NEWQD) (originally based on four quick-turn loads per HAS).

hazard classification. Process by which hazardous materials are assigned to one of the nine United Nations (UN) -recognized classes of dangerous goods.

hazardous debris distance. Distance at which the areal number density of hazardous debris becomes one per 600 square feet (ft^2) [55.7 square meters (m^2)].

hazardous fragment distance. Distance at which the areal number density of hazardous fragments or debris becomes one per 600 ft^2 [55.7 m^2].

hazardous fragment or debris. Fragments or debris having an impact energy of 58 ft-lbs [79 joule (J)] or greater.

hazards of electromagnetic radiation to ordnance (HERO). Situations in which transmitting equipment (e.g., radios, radar, electronic countermeasures, electronic counter-countermeasures, or ground penetrating radar) or other electromagnetic emitting devices can generate radiation of sufficient magnitude to induce or otherwise couple electromagnetic energy sufficient to exceed specified safety and/or reliability margins in EIDs contained within ordnance, or cause radiation-induced damage or degradation of performance in military munitions containing EID. (Also see Reference (f).)

HD. A division or subdivision denoting the character and predominant hazard within UN Classes 1, 2, 4, 5, and 6.

HE. An explosive substance designed to function by detonation (e.g., main charge, booster, or primary explosive.

headwall. An ECM's front wall. It is a critical feature that is directly associated with the strength designation assigned to an ECM.

heavy armor. Main battle tanks or other vehicles that are expected to contain fragments and reduce blast overpressure generated from an internal explosion of its AE stores.

HE equivalence. See "equivalent explosive weight."

high performance magazine. An earth-bermed, 2-story, box-shaped structure with internal non-propagation walls designed to reduce the MCE.

high pressure closure. See closure block.

holding yard. A temporary holding location for railcars, trucks, trailers, or shipping containers before storage or transportation.

hybrid propellant. A propellant charge using a combination of physically separated solid and liquid (or gelled) substances as fuel and oxidizer.

hygroscopic. A tendency of material to absorb moisture from its surroundings.

hypergolic. A property of various combinations of chemicals to self-ignite upon contact with each other without a spark or other external initiation source.

IMD. Distance to be maintained between two AE storage locations.

inhabited building distance (IBD). Distance to be maintained between a PES and an inhabited building.

inhabited buildings. Structures, other than AE-related buildings, occupied by personnel or the general public, both within and outside DoD establishments (e.g., schools, churches, residences, quarters, Service clubs, aircraft passenger terminals, stores, shops, factories, hospitals, theaters, mess halls, post offices, or post exchanges).

inspection station. A designated location at which trucks and railcars containing AE are inspected.

installation-related personnel. Military personnel (to include family members), DoD employees, DoD contractor personnel, and other personnel having either a direct operational (military or other Federal personnel undergoing training at an installation) or logistical support (e.g., vendors) relationship with installation activities.

integral air terminal LPS. An LPS that has strike termination devices mounted on the structure to be protected. The strike termination devices are connected to the earth electrode system via down conductors.

interchange yard. An area on a DoD installation set aside for exchanging railroad cars or vehicles with a common carrier.

interim holding facility (IHF). A temporary storage facility designed to hold recovered chemical warfare material (RCWM).

intraline distance. The distance to be maintained between any two AE-related buildings or sites within an AE related operating line.

joint DoD–non-DoD use runway or taxiway. A runway or taxiway serving both DoD and commercial aircraft. A runway or taxiway serving solely the Department of Defense, DoD-chartered, or non-DoD aircraft on DoD authorized business is not joint use.

joint hazard classification system (JHCS). A database containing hazard classification and safety data for DoD AE.

joint storage. AE storage in a facility that includes both DoD-titled and non-DoD-titled AE. In other than ownership, the stored AE items are similar.

K-factor. The factor in the formula $D=KW^{1/3}$ used in QD determinations where D represents distance in ft and W is the net explosive weight (NEW) in lbs. The K-factor is a constant and represents the degree of protection that is provided.

land use controls. Physical, legal, or administrative mechanisms that restrict the use of, or limit access to, real property, to manage risks to human health and the environment. Physical mechanisms encompass a variety of engineered remedies to contain or reduce contamination, or physical barriers to limit access to real property, such as fences or signs.

launch pad. The load-bearing base, apron, or platform upon which a rocket, missile, or space vehicle and its launcher rest prior to launch.

liquid propellant. Energetic liquids used for propulsion or operating power for missiles, rockets, AE, and other related devices.

loading density (w). Quantity of explosive per unit volume expressed as lbs/cubic feet (ft^3) [kg/cubic meter (m^3)].

loading docks. Facilities, structures, or paved areas used for transferring AE between modes of transportation.

long-term management. The period of site management (including maintenance, monitoring, record keeping, 5-year reviews, etc.) initiated after response (removal or remedial) objectives have been met (i.e., after Response Complete).

lunch room. A facility where meals may be distributed by food service personnel or brought by operating personnel for consumption. It may serve more than one PES.

magazine. Any building or structure used exclusively for the storage of AE.

marshalling yard. A designated area near a port facility where a unit or activity consolidates their equipment and prepares for movement.

mass explosion. Explosion that affects almost the entire quantity of AE virtually instantaneously.

mast LPS. An LPS consisting of one or more poles with a strike termination device connected to an earth electrode system by down conductors. Its purpose is to intercept lightning flashes and provide a zone of protection.

maximum fragment distance. The calculated maximum distance to which any fragment from the cylindrical portion of an AE case is expected to be thrown by the design mode detonation of a single AE item. This distance does not address fragments produced by sections of nose plugs, base plates, boat tails, or lugs. These special fragments, from the non-cylindrical portions of the AE case, can travel to significantly greater distances (i.e., more than 10,000 ft [3,048 m]) than the calculated maximum distances. The maximum fragment distance may also be the measured distance, based on testing, to which any fragment from an AE item is thrown.

MCE. In hazards evaluation, the MCE from a hypothesized accidental explosion, fire, or toxic chemical agent release (with explosives contribution) is the worst single event that is likely to occur from a given quantity and disposition of AE. The event must be realistic with a reasonable probability of occurrence considering the explosion propagation, burning rate characteristics, and physical protection given to the items involved. The MCE evaluated on this basis may then be used as a basis for effects calculations and casualty predictions. For HD 1.2.1, the MCE is expressed as a weight that is the product of the NEWQD and either the number of AE that reacts virtually instantaneously in the Sympathetic Reaction or Liquid Fuel/External Fire tests, or the number of AE in three unpalletized, outer shipping packages. The authorized MCE for a specific HD 1.2.1 item is listed in the JHCS.

MDAS. MPPEH that has been assessed and documented as not presenting an explosive hazard and for which the chain of custody has been established and maintained. This material is no longer considered to be MPPEH

MDEH. MPPEH that cannot be documented as MDAS, that has been assessed and documented as to the maximum explosive hazards the material is known or suspected to present, and for which the chain of custody has been established and maintained. This material is no longer considered to be MPPEH.

military munitions. Defined in section 101(e)(4) of Reference (e).

military munitions burial site. A site, regardless of location, where military munitions or CA, regardless of configuration, were intentionally buried, with the intent to abandon or discard. This term includes burial sites used to dispose of military munitions or CA, regardless of configuration, in a manner consistent with applicable environmental laws and regulations or the national practice at the time of burial. It does not include sites where munitions were intentionally covered with earth during authorized destruction by detonation, or where *in situ* capping is implemented as an engineered remedy under an authorized response action.

minimum separation distance. Minimum distance between a PES and personnel, assets, or structures required to provide the appropriate level of protection from a detonation (either intentional or unintentional) at the PES.

mitigation. A feature that reduces, limits, or controls the consequences of an AE reaction.

module. See barricaded open storage module.

MPPEH. Material that, prior to determination of its explosives safety status, potentially contains explosives or munitions (e.g., munitions containers and packaging material; munitions debris remaining after munitions use, demilitarization, or disposal; and range-related debris); or potentially contains a high enough concentration of explosives such that the material presents an explosive hazard (e.g., equipment, drainage systems, holding tanks, piping, or ventilation ducts that were associated with munitions production, demilitarization or disposal operations). Excluded from MPPEH are munitions within the DoD established munitions management system and other hazardous items that may present explosion hazards (e.g., gasoline cans, compressed gas cylinders) that are not munitions and are not intended for use as munitions.

munition with the greatest fragmentation distance. The munition with the greatest fragment distance that is reasonably expected (based on research or characterization) to be encountered in any particular area.

munitions and explosives of concern (MEC). A term distinguishing specific categories of military munitions that may pose unique explosives safety risks:

UXO, as defined in section 101(e)(5) of Reference (e).

DMM, as defined in section 2710(e)(2) of Reference (e); or

munitions consituent (e.g., TNT, cyclotrimethylenetrinitramine (RDX)), as defined in section 2710(e)(3) of Reference (e), present in high enough concentrations to pose an explosive hazard.

munitions constituent (MC). See section 2710(e)(3) of Reference (e). Generally, any materials originating from UXO, DMM, or other military munitions, including explosive and nonexplosive materials, and emission, degradation, or breakdown elements of such ordnance or munitions.

munitions debris. Remnants of munitions (e.g., fragments, penetrators, projectiles, shell casings, links, fins) remaining after munitions use, demilitarization, or disposal.

munitions response. Response actions, including investigation, removal actions, and remedial actions to address the explosives safety, human health, or environmental risks presented by UXO, DMM, or MC, or to support a determination that no removal or remedial action is required.

munitions response area (MRA). Any area on a defense site that is known or suspected to contain UXO, DMM, or MC. Examples include former ranges and munitions burial areas. A munitions response area is comprised of one or more munitions response sites.

munitions response site. A discrete location within an MRA that is known to require a munitions response.

navigable streams. Those parts of streams, channels, or canals capable of being used in their ordinary or maintained condition as highways of commerce over which trade and travel are, or may be, conducted in the customary modes. Streams that are not capable of navigation by barges, tugboats, and other large vessels are not included, unless they are used extensively and regularly for the operation of pleasure boats.

net explosive quantity (NEQ). NEW expressed in kg.

<u>NEW</u>. The total weight of all explosives substances (i.e., high explosive weight (HEW), propellant weight, and pyrotechnic weight) in the AE, expressed in lbs. NEW is used for transportation purposes.

<u>NEWQD</u>. The total weight, expressed in lbs [kg], of all explosive substances (HEW, propellant weight, and pyrotechnic weight) in the AE, unless testing has been conducted to support an approved different value due to the contribution of HEs, propellants, or pyrotechnics. For all HD 1.3 or 1.4 (other than CG S) AE, NEWQD is equal to NEW. NEWQD is used when applying QD and other criteria in this document.

<u>nitrogen padding (or blanket)</u>. The nitrogen filled void or ullage of a closed container used to prevent oxidation or to avoid formation of a flammable mixture, or a nitrogen atmosphere in or around an operation or piece of equipment.

<u>non-combustible construction</u>. Construction that uses materials that do not readily ignite and burn when exposed to fire (e.g., concrete, masonry, and metal structures).

<u>non-DoD entity</u>. An entity (government, private, or corporate) that is not part of a DoD Component.

<u>non-DoD explosives operations and storage</u>. Explosives operations or storage conducted on DoD property, but not under DoD oversight. (See DoD explosives operations and storage.)

<u>non-essential personnel</u>. Individuals, as identified by the DoD Component, not associated with an AE operation.

<u>non-robust munitions</u>

For purposes of determining SG, non-robust munitions are those HD 1.1 and HD 1.2 military munitions that are not categorized as SG 1, SG 3, SG 4, or SG 5. Examples of such munitions include torpedoes and underwater mines. (See also "SG.")

For purposes of determining case fragment distances for intentional detonations, non-robust munitions are those military munitions that do not meet the second definition (definition 2) of robust munitions. (See also "robust munitions.")

<u>on-call construction support</u>. Construction support provided, on an as-needed basis, where the probability of encountering UXO, other munitions that may have experienced abnormal environments (e.g., DMM), MC in high enough concentrations to pose an explosive hazard, or CA, regardless of configuration, has been determined to be low. This support can respond from offsite when called, or be onsite and available to provide required construction support.

<u>one percent lethality distance</u>. A distance calculated from a given CA MCE and meteorological conditions (temperature, wind speed, Pasquill stability factor) and established as the distance at which dosage from that MCE agent release would be 150 milligrams per minute (mg-min)/m^3 for H and HD agents, 75 mg-min/m^3 for HT agent, 150 mg-min/m^3 for L, 10 mg-min/m^3 for

isopropyl methylphosphonofluoridate (GB) agent, 4.3 mg-min/m^3 for 0-ethyl S-[2-(diisopropylamino) ethyl] methylphosphonothioate (VX) vapor, and 0.1 mg-min/m^3 for inhalation and deposition of liquid VX.

onsite construction support. Dedicated construction support, where the probability of encountering UXO, other munitions that may have experienced abnormal environments (e.g., DMM), MC in high enough concentrations to pose an explosive hazard, or CA, regardless of configuration, has been determined to be moderate to high.

on-the-surface. A situation in which UXO, DMM, or CA, regardless of configuration, are either entirely or partially exposed above the ground surface (i.e., the top of the soil layer), or entirely or partially exposed above the surface of a water body (e.g., because of tidal activity).

open burn. An open-air combustion process by which excess, unserviceable, or obsolete munitions are destroyed to eliminate their inherent explosive hazards.

open detonation. An open-air process used for the treatment of excess, unserviceable, or obsolete munitions whereby an explosive donor charge initiates the munitions being treated.

operating building *or location*. Any *site, facility, or* structure, except a magazine, in which operations associated with AE are conducted (e.g., manufacturing, processing, handling, loading, or assembling).

operating line. A group of buildings, facilities, or related workstations so arranged as to permit performance of the consecutive steps of operations associated with AE (e.g., manufacture, loading, assembly, modification, or maintenance).

operational range. See section 101(e)(3) of Reference (e). Also includes "military range," "active range," and "inactive range" as those terms are defined in part 266.201 of Reference (d).

operational shield. A barrier constructed at a particular location or around a particular machine or operating station to protect personnel, material, or equipment from the effects of a localized fire or explosion.

ordnance. Explosives, chemicals, pyrotechnics, and similar stores (e.g., bombs, guns and ammunition, flares, smoke, or napalm). (See military munitions.)

packaging, inner and outer. Material used to surround and protect substances and articles during transportation and storage. They are generally made of lightweight materials such as fiberboard or fiberglass.

passenger railroad. Any steam, diesel, electric, or other railroad that carries passengers for hire.

PES. The location of a quantity of AE that will create a blast, fragment, thermal, or debris hazard in the event of an accidental explosion of its contents.

pier. A landing place or platform built into the water, perpendicular or oblique to the shore, for the berthing of vessels.

portal barricade. A barricade placed in front of an entrance into an underground storage facility. Its function is to reflect that portion of the shock wave moving directly outward from the entrance, thereby, reducing the pressures along the extended tunnel axis and increasing the pressures in the opposite direction. The result is a more circular IBD area centered at the portal.

primary explosives. Highly sensitive compounds that are typically used in detonators and primers. A reaction is easily triggered by heat, spark, impact, or friction. Examples of primary explosives are lead azide and mercury fulminate.

primary fragment. A fragment from material in intimate contact with reacting AE.

prohibited area. A designated area at airfields, seadromes, or heliports where AE facilities are prohibited.

propagation. Transfer of a reaction between AE.

public access exclusion distance (PAED). The longest distance of the hazardous fragment distance (HFD), IBD for overpressure, or the one percent lethality distance. For siting purposes, the PAED is analogous to the IBD for explosives; therefore, personnel not directly associated with the chemical operations are not to be allowed within the PAED.

public exclusion distance. The calculated distance from the toxic chemical agent source at which no more than 10.0, 4.3, and 150 mg-min/m^3 is present for GB, VX, and mustard, respectively, or the explosives safety IBD, whichever is greater.

public traffic route (PTR). Any public street, road, highway, navigable stream, or passenger railroad, including roads on a military reservation used routinely by the general public for through traffic.

public traffic route distance (PTRD). Distance to be maintained between a PES and a PTR exposure.

~~pyrotechnic material. Common name for a magnesium-incendiary mixture with an agent symbol of "PT."~~

QD. The quantity of explosive material and distance separation relationships that provide defined levels of protection. The relationships are based on levels of risk considered acceptable for specific exposures and are tabulated in applicable QD tables. These separation distances do not provide absolute safety or protection. Greater distances than those in the QD tables should be used if practical.

qualified receiver. Individuals or entities that have personnel who are trained and experienced in the identification and safe handling of used and unused military munitions, and any known or potential explosive hazards that may be associated with the MPPEH they receive; and are licensed and permitted or otherwise qualified to receive, manage, and process MPPEH.

quantitative risk assessment. Estimating the probability of fatality (individual risk) and the expected number of fatalities (group risk) based on the product of the probability of the event, the probability of fatality given the event, and the exposure, and comparing those risks with approved criteria.

range. Defined in section 101(e)(1) of Reference (e).

range activities. Defined in section 101(e)(2) of Reference (e).

range clearance. The destruction or removal and proper disposition of used military munitions (e.g., UXO and munitions debris) and other range-related debris (e.g., target debris, military munitions packaging and crating material) to maintain or enhance operational range safety or prevent the accumulation of such material from impairing or preventing operational range use. Does not include removal, treatment, or remediation of chemical residues or munitions constituents from environmental media, or actions to address discarded military munitions (e.g., burial pits) on operational ranges.

range-related debris. Debris, other than munitions debris, collected from operational ranges or from former ranges (e.g., target debris, military munitions packaging and crating material).

RCWM. CWM used for its intended purpose or previously disposed of as waste, which has been discovered during a CWM response or by chance (e.g., accidental discovery by a member of the public), that the Department of Defense has either secured in place or placed under DoD control, normally in a DDESB-approved storage location or interim holding facility, pending final disposition.

ready ammunition storage. A location where AE is stored for near-term tactical or training use.

real property. Lands, buildings, structures, utilities systems, improvements, and appurtenances thereto. Includes equipment attached to and made part of buildings and structures (such as heating systems) but not moveable equipment (such as plant equipment).

reduced QD magazine. A containment structure that through full-scale testing has demonstrated its ability to contain or significantly control explosion effects (i.e., fragmentation, overpressure, thermal) associated with an internal explosion involving 125 percent of the magazine's rated NEWQD capacity, and has been approved by the DDESB for application of reduced QD.

risk. The product of the probability or frequency that an accident will occur within a certain time and the accident's consequences to people, property or the environment.

risk-based evaluation distance. The distance from a PES where probability of fatality (P_f) (individual risk) is equal to 1×10^{-8} for an individual present 24/7/365 in the open or IBD, whichever is greater (i.e., the distance from a PES within which all exposures [ES group] must be evaluated for a risk-based site plan). (See ES group.)

robust munitions

For purposes of determining SG, robust munitions are those HD 1.1 and HD 1.2 military munitions that meet two of the following criteria:

Have a ratio of the explosive weight to empty case weight less than 1.

Have a nominal wall thickness of at least 0.4 inches [10 mm].

Have a case thickness/$NEW^{1/3}$ greater than 0.05 inches/$lb^{1/3}$ [0.165 cm/$kg^{1/3}$]. Examples of robust munitions include 20-mm, 25-mm, and 30-mm cartridges, general purpose bombs, artillery projectiles, and penetrator warheads. (See also "SG.")

For purposes of determining case fragment distances for intentional detonations, robust munitions are those that meet the definition above or meet the definition of fragmenting military munitions. (See also extremely heavy case munitions and fragmenting military munitions.)

rock strength. Designations (e.g., strong, moderately strong, or weak rock) providing a general classification of rock types.

roll-on/roll-off (RORO). An AE movement that is essentially an extension of the basic transportation process involving the movement, without lifting, of AE-laden wheeled conveyances into or from a transporter (e.g., a barge), such that the conveyances remain in a continuous transportation mode through a transshipment point.

RSP. The portion of EOD procedures that involves the application of special disposal methods or tools to interrupt the functioning or otherwise defeat the firing train of UXO from triggering an unacceptable detonation.

runway. Any surface on land designated for aircraft takeoff and landing operations, or a designated lane of water for takeoff and landing operations of seaplanes.

secondary explosives. For the purposes of this document, secondary explosives are generally less sensitive to initiation than primary explosives and are typically used in booster and main charge applications. A severe shock is usually required to trigger a reaction. Examples are TNT, RDX or cyclonite, cyclotetramethylene-tetranitramine (HMX) (also known as octogen), and tetryl.

secondary fragment. Fragments produced by the impact of primary fragments or airblast into surrounding structures, AE, or earth.

<u>Secretarial exemptions or certifications</u>. A written authorization granted by the Secretary of a Military Department for strategic or other compelling reasons that permits long-term noncompliance with a mandatory requirement of DoD explosives safety criteria.

<u>secure explosives holding area</u>. Defined in chapter 205 of Defense Transportation Regulation 4500.9-R (Reference (i)).

<u>secure nonexplosives holding area</u>. Defined in chapter 205 of Reference (i).

<u>service magazine</u>. A building of an operating line used for the intermediate storage of AE.

<u>SG</u>

A category used to describe the susceptibility of HD 1.1 and HD 1.2 military munitions to sympathetic detonation (SD) for the purpose of storage within a high performance magazine (HPM), or where ARMCO, Inc., revetments or substantial dividing walls are used to reduce MCE. Each HD 1.1 and HD 1.2 military munition is designated, based on its physical attributes, into one of five SGs, which can be found in the JHCS; directed energy weapons are further identified by assigning the suffix "D" following the SG designation. The SGs are:

<u>SG 1 – robust munitions</u>. (See robust munitions.)

<u>SG 2 – non-robust munitions</u>. (See non-robust munitions.)

<u>SG 3 – fragmenting military munitions</u>. (See fragmenting military munitions.)

<u>SG 4 – CBU weapons</u>. (See CBU military munitions.)

<u>SG 5 – SD sensitive military munitions</u>. Munitions for which HPM non-propagation walls are not effective. Military munitions are assigned to SG 5 when either very sensitive to propagation or the sensitivity has not been determined.

For purposes of determining case fragment distances for intentional detonations, SG 1 items will be either robust or extremely heavy case munitions; SG 3 items are considered robust munitions; and SG 2, SG 4, and SG 5 military munitions are considered non-robust munitions.

<u>shared launch facility</u>. Any space or orbital launch facility supporting both DoD and non-DoD launch services and operations, as determined by the DoD Component involved or by mutual agreement when multiple DoD Components are involved.

<u>ship or barge units</u>. Combination of AE ships (including submarines at berth), barges, or piers or wharves not separated by required IMD.

<u>sideflash</u>. The phenomenon where lightning current will arc through a non-conductive medium in order to attach to other objects. An electrical spark caused by differences of potential that

occurs between conductive metal bodies or between such metal bodies and a component of the LPS or earth electrode system.

single-chamber storage site. An excavated chamber with its own access to the natural ground surface that is not connected to any other storage chamber.

small arms ammunition. Ammunition, without projectiles that contain explosives (other than tracers), that is .50 caliber or smaller, or for shotguns.

source emission limits. The amount of toxic chemical agent that may be released at a particular point that allows for natural dilution, ventilation, and meteorological conditions.

spall. The material broken loose from any surface of an acceptor chamber or cell by a shock wave transmitted through the wall. Spall is also used to describe this process.

standoff distance. Minimum separation required between a wall or barrier and the edge of a stack of AE.

static missile battery. Deployed ground-based missiles meant to be employed in a non-mobile mission for offensive or defensive purposes.

static test stand. Locations where liquid energetic engines or solid propellant motors are tested in place.

strike termination device or system. A component or feature of an LPS intended to intercept lightning strikes. They may include overhead wires or grids, air terminals, or a building's grounded structural elements.

support facilities. Facilities that support AE operations (e.g., field offices, AE support equipment maintenance, forklift charging stations, dunnage storage, or inert storage buildings).

surge suppression or protection. The attenuation, suppression, or diversion of lightning-induced electrical energy to ground.

suspect truck and railcar holding areas. A designated location for placing motor vehicles or railcars either containing AE that are suspected of being in a hazardous condition or motor vehicles or railcars that may be in a condition that is hazardous to the AE.

sympathetic detonation (SD). The detonation of AE produced by the detonation of adjacent AE.

tactical facilities. Prepared locations with an assigned combat mission (e.g., missile launch facilities, alert aircraft parking areas, or fixed gun positions).

taxiway. Any surface designated as such in the basic airfield clearance criteria specified by a DoD Component publication or Federal Aviation Regulation.

team separation distance. The distance that munitions response teams must be separated from each other during munitions response activities involving intrusive operations.

technology-aided surface removal. A removal of UXO, DMM, or CWM on the surface (i.e., the top of the soil layer) only, in which the detection process is primarily performed visually, but is augmented by technology aids (e.g., hand-held magnetometers or metal detectors) because vegetation, the weathering of UXO, DMM, or CWM, or other factors make visual detection difficult.

time critical removal action. Generally, removal actions where, based on the site evaluation, a determination is made that a removal is appropriate, and that fewer than 6 months exists before onsite removal activity must begin.

TNT equivalence. See equivalent explosive weight.

toxic chemical agent. A substance intended for military use with lethal or incapacitating effects on personnel through its chemical properties. Excluded from toxic chemical agents for purposes of this document are riot control agents, chemical herbicides, smoke- and flame-producing items, and individual dissociated components of toxic chemical agent munitions.

toxic chemical agent accident. Any unintentional or uncontrolled release of a toxic chemical agent when:

Reportable damage occurs to property from contamination, or costs are incurred for decontamination.

Individuals exhibit physiological symptoms of toxic chemical agent exposure.

The toxic chemical agent quantity released to the atmosphere is such that a serious potential for exposure is created by exceeding the applicable AEL for unprotected workers or the general public or property.

toxic chemical agent MCE. The hypothesized maximum quantity of toxic chemical agent that could be accidentally released from AE without explosive contribution, bulk container, or process as a result of a single unintended, unplanned, or accidental occurrence. It must be realistic with a reasonable probability of occurrence.

toxic chemical munitions. Defined in section 266.201 of Reference (d) and section 1521(j)(1) of title 50, U.S.C. (Reference (j)).

Ufer ground. An earth electrode system that consists of solid conductors encased along the bottom of a concrete foundation footing or floor and is in direct contact with earth.

underground storage facility. May consist of a single chamber or a series of connected chambers and other protective construction features. The chambers may be either excavated or natural geological cavities.

United States. The 50 States, the District of Columbia, the Commonwealth of Puerto Rico, the U.S. Virgin Islands, Guam, American Samoa, and the Commonwealth of the Northern Mariana Islands, Johnston Atoll, Kingman Reef, Midway Island, Nassau Island, Palmyra Island, Wake Island, and any other territory or possession over which the United States has jurisdiction, and associated navigable waters, contiguous zones, and ocean waters of which the natural resources are under the exclusive management authority of the United States.

UXO. Defined in section 101(e)(5) of Reference (e).

UXO-qualified personnel. Personnel who have performed successfully in military EOD positions, or are qualified to perform in the following Department of Labor, Service Contract Act, Directory of Occupations, contractor positions: UXO Technician II, UXO Technician III, UXO Safety Officer, UXO Quality Control Specialist, or Senior UXO Supervisor.

UXO technicians. Personnel who are qualified for and filling Department of Labor, Service Contract Act, Directory of Occupations, contractor positions of UXO Technician I, UXO Technician II, and UXO Technician III.

vent. Expose any internal cavities of MPPEH, to include training or practice munitions (e.g., concrete bombs), using DDESB or DoD Component-approved procedures, to confirm that an explosive hazard is not present.

vulnerable construction. Buildings of vulnerable construction (e.g., schools, high-rise buildings, restaurants, large warehouse-type retail stores) of which there are three main types:

Buildings of curtain wall construction that have four stories or more and are constructed with external non-load bearing panels on a separate sub-frame that are supported off the structural frame or floors for the full height of the building.

Buildings of largely glass construction that have four stories or more and have at least 50 percent of their wall areas glazed.

Any large building that employs non-load-bearing cladding panels.

waiver. A written authorization granted by the proper authority within a DoD Component for strategic or other compelling reasons that permits a temporary deviation from a mandatory requirement of DoD explosives safety criteria.

waste military munition. Defined in part 266.202 of Reference (d).

wharf. A landing place or platform built into the water or along the shore for the berthing of vessels.

wharf yard. An AE area close to a pier or wharf where railcars or trucks are temporarily held in support of pier or wharf operations.

wholly inert. Those munitions (e.g., dummy) or munitions components (e.g., ogive, rotating band, adapter, lifting plugs) that have never contained reactive materials (i.e., explosives, chemical agents, or chemicals, such as pyrophoric chemicals). Once an inert item is employed as a component of a military munition, it may no longer be considered wholly inert.

wingwall. A wall located on either side of an ECM's headwall. It may slope to the ground or may join a wingwall from an adjacent ECM. It may be monolithic (of single construction) or separated by expansion joints from the headwall. The purpose of a wingwall is to retain the earth fill along the side slope of an ECM.

with its means of initiation. An AE item with its normal initiating device, such as a detonator or detonating fuze, assembled to it or packed with it, and this device is considered to present a significant risk during storage and transport, but not one great enough to be unacceptable.

without means of initiation. An AE item without its normal initiating device assembled to it or packed with it. The term also applies to an AE item packed with its initiating device, provided the device is packed so as to eliminate the risk of causing detonation of the AE item in the event of accidental functioning of the initiating device. In addition, the term applies to an AE item assembled with its initiating device, provided there are protective features such that the initiating device is very unlikely to cause detonation of the AE item under conditions that are associated with storage and transport. For hazard classification purposes, a means of initiation that possesses two independent effective protective features is not considered to present a significant risk of causing the detonation of an AE item under conditions associated with storage and transport.

zone of protection. The space beneath the LPS that is substantially immune to direct lightning.